BASKETBALL HALL OF FAMERS

BILL RUSSELL

Chris Hayhurst

the rosen publishing group's
rosen
central

Published in 2002 by The Rosen Publishing Group, Inc.
29 East 21st Street, New York, NY 10010

Copyright © 2002 by The Rosen Publishing Group, Inc.

First Edition

Library of Congress Cataloging-in-Publication Data

Hayhurst, Chris.
Bill Russell / by Chris Hayhurst.
p. cm. – (Basketball Hall of Famers)
Includes bibliographical references (p.   ) and index.
Summary: A biography of the Boston Celtics basketball player
who became the first African American inducted into the
Basketball Hall of Fame.
ISBN 0-8239-3480-2 (library binding)
1. Russell, Bill, 1934– —Juvenile literature. 2. Basketball
players—United States—Biography—Juvenile literature.
[1. Russell, Bill, 1934– 2. Basketball players. 3. African
Americans—Biography.]
I. Title. II. Series.
GV884.R86 H39 2001
796.323'092–dc21

2001004614

Manufactured in the United States of America

contents

introduction

Fans of basketball know their game. They know that the players are, for the most part, massive. Seven-foot, 300-pound men slam-dunk the ball through the hoop. Young, lean players dribble behind their backs, throw no-look passes to teammates, and leap through the air to snag rebounds, block shots, and sink three-pointers while stressed-out coaches pace frantically up and down the sidelines. Games are often won or lost on a single play, or on one desperate shot that either swishes through the net or rattles off the rim.

These days, the National Basketball Association (NBA) is the definition of "hip." Players make rap albums and wear the latest

Bill Russell, who led the Boston Celtics to eleven championships, was once called the "game's greatest living legend" by Michael Jordan.

styles. The biggest stars play roles in movies, write books about their lives, do lengthy interviews for television and print journalists, and start their own lines of clothing. Off the court, they wear expensive suits and drive fast cars. They own enormous houses. They live the lifestyles of millionaire celebrities—always in the public eye and often followed, idolized, and scrutinized.

What many fans of the NBA fail to realize is that this show—including the fame, stardom, wealth, and tremendous talent—has been unfolding for some time. It didn't just happen overnight. Before basketball heroes and teams were known by last names or nicknames alone—Jordan, Iverson, Shaq, and Stockton; the Bulls, the Magic, the Raptors, and the Rockets—there were dozens of other major players and teams. There was Wilt Chamberlain, one of the all-time best scorers in the history of the game. There was Earl "the Pearl" Monroe, who was so utterly elusive, and so devastatingly effective on the court, that opposing players swore he played like a ghost, elevating to the hoop at will, and dropping the ball through the net like he was alone on the court. There were many others, too. You'll find most of them in the NBA Hall of Fame, recognized for their achievements both on and off the court, as basketball players and as human beings.

One player in particular, however, stands out to this day. His name is William Felton Russell. In fact, Russell's contribution to the game of basketball was so great and so far reaching that Michael Jordan once called him "the game's greatest living legend," and went on to say that "no one has influenced the game of basketball more than Bill." *Sports Illustrated* magazine recently declared Russell "the greatest team player on the greatest team [the Boston Celtics] of all time." Cable television network HBO named him "The Greatest Winner of the Twentieth Century." And, in 1980, before Jordan entered the scene, the Professional Basketball Writers Association of

America voted Russell the "Greatest Player in the History of the NBA."

Sportswriters have often named Russell to their lists of all-time greats, not only as a testament to his playing style, but also because he was such a team player. "No athlete ever had such a positive influence on his teammates— everybody was a better player when Bill Russell was on their side," said Richard Hoffer in a 1999 *Sports Illustrated* article.

There's no doubt about it: William Russell—veteran NBA center, five-time NBA Most Valuable Player, twelve-time all-star, Hall of Famer, and, most important, leader of eleven championship-winning Celtics teams over his thirteen seasons—knew the game of basketball well, especially when it came to defensive play. But he also happened to know life as a black man at a time when African Americans lacked the same fundamental rights as whites. He knew what prejudice was, and fought it in his own unique way. He wrote books about his life and his experiences and was not afraid to speak out about the issues he supported, or with which he disagreed. He broke new ground for African Americans all over the country, first as a basketball player, then as an NBA coach, and, finally, as a U.S. citizen. The truth is that Russell did more for basketball than did any other player in the history of the game; his influence, felt at every tip-off and throughout the entirety of every one of today's games, is undeniable. His story is a remarkable one.

Despite the crushing environment of segregation, Bill Russell's strong family ties and his parents' pride helped him succeed in life.

William's father, Charles Russell, was a big man. Standing six feet two inches tall and weighing more than 200 pounds, "Mister Charlie," as he was known, was uneducated, but he worked hard in a nearby factory making paper bags. He was strong, athletic, and built like an ox, and when he was around—especially as the boys grew older and became more mischievous—there was no doubt who was in charge.

William's mother, Katie Russell, was no pushover, either. A high school dropout, she was determined to send her children to college. As Russell recalled years later in an autobiography, *Second Wind*, Katie "was rich, tender and strong all at once. If I'd run into a king or a queen, I would have been proud to show my mother off to them."

But there was no royalty in Monroe in the 1930s; in fact, quite the opposite was true. Poverty ruled, and the Russell family was no exception to its devastating effects. Despite William's father's hard work at the factory, there was very little money to cover expenses and no sign that things would change. Charles Russell had, as it's called, a dead-end job, and he knew it.

William's parents had only one choice, and that was to leave Monroe and its sluggish economy and racist attitudes behind. They knew that, in order to secure a better future for their sons, one in which they would get the education and the opportunities they needed to succeed, the family would have to move to a better environment.

Temporarily leaving his wife and sons behind, Charles Russell boarded a train to Michigan and began the search for a new home. In Detroit, he nearly found what he was looking for—a decent job in a factory making machinery for World War II—but decided that the northern cold was too much to endure. He packed his bags again and embarked for sunny California. There, in the city of Oakland, he made up his mind: This was the place.

Before long, Charles Russell sent for his family. Unsure of what awaited them, Katie and the boys were on a train heading west.

California Dreaming

To William, Oakland was a much better place than Monroe could ever become. The weather was beautiful. Outright segregation was far less common. Blacks had rights similar to those of whites. Cole Elementary, where he and his brother went to school, was a world apart from the school they had attended in Louisiana. "We had real desks and teachers for each grade," wrote Russell, "and all kinds of studies and activities that so excited my mother that she'd make me tell her everything when I came home every day." Life, at least compared to what it used to be, was very good indeed.

But it certainly wasn't perfect. Racism was still prevalent all over the country, and Oakland was no exception. There was tension

Bill Russell's dominance as a rebounder and a shot blocker forced the NBA and its fans to judge players as much for their defensive skills as for their scoring abilities.

between blacks and whites, and sometimes that strain exploded into violence and riots. Even children, who should have had no part in the conflict, were often in danger. In another autobiography, *Go Up for Glory*, Russell recalled what it was like being a black boy in a big city: "You are little, but you learn fast. Be off the street by five o'clock. Move fast if you are little and black. Keep moving, because the police will get you, and book you, and maybe kick you because you are black." Later, in an interview with *Sports Illustrated*, Russell said, "I couldn't even go downtown. The cops would chase the black kids away."

When they first moved to the city, the Russells lived in Oakland's public housing projects—buildings funded federally or by the state that are erected for housing the poor—in an impoverished part of town known as Landlord's Paradise. Their house had eight rooms and a garage, but it also had eight other families living in it. There were pigs, sheep, and chickens running around in the yard, and everything was filthy and falling apart. All their landlord cared about was money. Nothing was ever repaired, and living conditions were absolutely terrible.

The neighborhood wasn't exactly friendly, either. Soon after they arrived, William was minding his own business outside his house when another boy came up to him, slapped him across the face, and then continued on his way as if nothing had occurred. He was shocked. Nine years old and the new kid on the block, William didn't know what to do. Then his mother, who had seen what had happened, came running out of the building. She grabbed her son and hustled him down the street until they caught up with the other child. There, in front of the instigator's friends, she made him fight the boy. The punches started flying.

It wasn't long before the fight was over. William had won. Thinking he was done, he turned to his mother. But Katie had other ideas. While her son was fighting, another boy in the group of onlookers said something Katie found offensive. He had no choice, she said, but to fight that boy, too. William didn't fare as well in the second bout, but he certainly learned his lesson. If he was ever going to earn the respect of his peers, he would have to stick up for himself. And if anyone so much as tried to push him around, it was up to him to sort things out. His mother wouldn't have it any other way.

Tragedy Strikes

Eventually, the Russells moved out of the eight-room house and into a different housing project near the boys' elementary school. Their new home was much cleaner and safer. It was even integrated, with blacks and whites living in the same building. They were moving up in the world.

While the boys went to school, the elder Russells worked hard to support them and save the money that would one day send their sons to college. They both found jobs in nearby ship-yards and one would work days while the other took the night shift. One parent was always home to watch the boys. Later, Charles Russell started his own small business, trucking produce from farms in the country to markets in Oakland. He was finally making decent money. The long hours in the paper mill seemed so far away.

One day, however, in the fall of 1946, that changed forever. When William got home from school, his mother was gone. Suddenly, for no apparent reason, she had become gravely ill. Her kidneys were failing. And now, at thirty-two years old, she was confined to a hospital bed and had just one or two weeks to live. The doctors could do nothing. Just like that, Katie was dead.

Charles Russell, William, and Charlie Jr. were in shock. In a matter of days, their world had been turned upside down. The strongest woman they knew had left them forever, and now they were nearly alone.

Mister Charlie, however, refused to let Katie's death divide his family. He and the boys brought their mother back to Louisiana and buried her with her relatives. Then, despite the concerns of family members, who thought the boys should stay in Louisiana where they could be raised properly, Charles Russell returned to Oakland with his sons. As Russell recalled years later in *Second Wind,* "He told everybody that we could make it ourselves, but they seemed doubtful." Charles Russell refused to give up on his and Katie's dream of sending their kids to college, and knew that the only way in which that dream would ever come true was if they remained in California. "We had to pull together," remembered Russell. "And being men, we couldn't afford to feel sorry for ourselves." William was only twelve years old.

Back in Oakland, Charles Russell had to quit his trucking job, which was too demanding for a single father with two kids to look after. He wanted to spend more time with his sons, to be closer to them, and to help them through school. He took a new job as a metal worker in a foundry and did the best he could.

McClymonds High

B asketball was really not a part of William's childhood—in fact, he was a lousy athlete.

All the family's natural athletic talent, it appeared, had gone to Charlie Jr., who was a truly gifted sportsman. Two years older than William, he took to athletics like a fish takes to water. He was so talented that he was recruited to Oakland Tech High School, which had an almost entirely white student body. In those days, that was a very big deal. William, up until this point, had only learned the basics of basketball by playing with friends on a makeshift court, and he certainly wasn't very serious about it.

William looked up to his brother Charlie, who was an excellent basketball player. But as he learned the game, he was painfully aware of the comparisons that were made between him and his brother. Inevitably, people always expressed their dismay at how the two boys could possibly be related—one with such a knack for sports and the other with no visible talent for them. But William refused to give up the game. He loved sports, although he wasn't coordinated.

William's woes began at Hoover Junior High. There, while his brother strutted his stuff at Oakland Tech, William never made the cut of any sports teams. Thinking a change of pace might be in order, he then tried out for the band as a clarinetist. But music, as it turned out, was not one of his strengths either. To make matters worse, William, a habitually lazy student, nearly failed to pass eighth grade.

High school, at least in the beginning, was no more promising. William entered McClymonds High, a public school with mostly black students, as a tenth-grader. He went out for the football team but was cut. He tried out for the pep squad team and was cut from it, too. Finally, he attempted to gain placement on the school's basketball team, but his results were no better.

William nearly gave up. He was doing better academically, because he had learned his lesson and picked up the pace when it came to studying, but everything else seemed impossible. Here he was, the younger brother of the city's most famous athletic hero, and he couldn't even *buy* a spot on a sports team.

Then one day, as he made his way to the gymnasium to shoot some hoops, he passed the school maintenance worker in the hall. The maintenance worker, who recognized William immediately, remarked that he hadn't seen him near the gym in a long time. He wanted to know why he wasn't practicing with the team. "These guys are just better than me," replied William. "I couldn't make it." The worker, a smart man, didn't buy it. "If you think so," he said, "then they always will be."

The maintenance worker's words of wisdom rang like a bell in William's ears. It was mind over matter. If he just kept a positive attitude, he was bound to improve.

Odd Man In

Soon after, in the fall of 1949, a turn of events took place that changed William's life forever. A man named George Powles, William's homeroom teacher at Hoover Junior High, had taken a job at McClymonds and was now serving as the high school junior varsity basketball coach. Powles, who was a white man, was one of the few teachers in the school who seemed to be color-blind. He treated his black students exactly the same way he treated his white students. And although many of the school's white teachers seemed to discourage black kids from even considering a college education, Powles was different. Everyone was equal in his eyes, and everyone, he felt, should have the chance for a higher education.

William respected this new coach, and when Powles approached him and suggested that he try out for his team, William gave it some thought. At first he wasn't sure. He knew what a wreck he was on the court and wasn't excited about making a fool of himself. But eventually he agreed to try again.

The tryouts were mostly predictable. William dropped passes, missed the easiest of shots, and, for the most part, stumbled all over himself. But something remarkable happened: He made the team. "I was terrible," recalled Russell. "But Powles had faith in me as a person and didn't want to break my spirit."

Powles couldn't bear to see William fail again, and decided to keep him on the team as the sixteenth player on a fifteen-man roster. William wouldn't even get his own uniform (he had to share one with another player). But this tall, thin, uncoordinated boy finally had a reason to be proud. Thanks to Powles, he could play ball. "By that one gesture," wrote Russell, "I believe that man saved me from becoming a juvenile delinquent. If I hadn't had basketball, all of my energies and frustrations would surely have been carried in some other direction."

William could not believe his good fortune. With newfound enthusiasm, he spent countless hours practicing and developing his skills. At team practices, he hustled as fast as he could. He played as though his life depended on it. He even entered into pick-up games after school at the local boys club, hoping the extra playing time would improve his game.

Cheers and Jeers

Despite the fact that he hardly ever got to play in actual games for the team, William almost always wore his heart on his sleeve when he did play. He felt determined to do his best at every single moment. Usually, however, the only playing time he earned was when the match was completely one-sided and there was no possibility that he could throw a game. Then, to the cheers—and jeers—of the crowd, he'd step in and make one bad play after another. It was ugly, but it was exactly what he needed.

With time, William's game improved. He played in more games, and for longer periods, and by the end of his junior year he was bumped up to McClymond's varsity team. He wouldn't be a starter right away, but that didn't matter. He had his own position and his own uniform. William Russell was now the third-string center.

The main reason William made the varsity team was his defensive skills. He had yet to develop a good shot, but his ability to jump was outstanding. Opposing players would shoot the ball and William would just jump up in the air and bat it away before it reached the hoop. He would stop ball after ball this way, leaping over again to swat, slap, snag, and bring down shots, rebounds, and passes.

Thanks to his well-planned defensive work, William landed the starting spot at center when his senior year rolled around. Still, his offensive skills were lagging, as were his

Bill Russell made such an impression on the court during high school that he eventually received a basketball scholarship from the University of San Francisco.

instincts. He was well over six feet tall and was gradually adapting to his growing body, but William lacked the aggression necessary to control other players on the court. He was a large guy, but he didn't know how to use his size to either his own or his team's advantage.

Senior year went well, and he began to come into his own as a distinctive player. Then, near the end of the season, not long before graduation, he suited up for what would become the biggest, most important game he had ever played. The contest was tight: Oakland High versus McClymonds High. Both teams were very good, with top-notch records and excellent players.

Playing in the center position for Oakland High opposite William was a well-known all-city center named Truman Bruce. Many people thought he was the best center the city had seen in years. William, however, was not intimidated, and to the disbelief of almost everyone in attendance, he proceeded to dominate Bruce from the opening tip-off to the very last whistle. He scored 14 points and blocked countless shots. He snagged nearly 20 rebounds. Bruce, on the other hand, was practically shut down.

William couldn't have timed this outburst better. As it turned out, there was a very important man in the stands from the University of San Francisco (USF) named Hal DeJulio. DeJulio, who had played ball at USF years before, had come to help out the Oakland High coach and to watch Bruce strut his stuff. He was hoping to convince Bruce to go to USF the following year to play for the USF Dons. But when he saw William play, he changed his mind. He'd take the Russell boy over Bruce any day.

Soon after that game, DeJulio offered William a USF scholarship to play basketball. William couldn't believe it and neither could Charles Russell. It was too good to be true. William—who at one point couldn't make a single basketball team, and who had planned to apprentice as a sheet-metal worker after high school to save money for college tuition—would play college ball. And, even better, his education would be sponsored.

In January 1951, William graduated from high school. During those years, his high school teams lost only three games in the three seasons he played. The team was also awarded Oakland's Keyes Memorial Trophy for the team that demonstrated the best sportsmanship.

On the Road

Before he could graduate with his classmates, William packed his bags and hit the road. He had been selected to play on a traveling all-star team of promising young players who finished school midyear. The team played all over the northwest United States and British Columbia, Canada, and won nearly every game. For William, the trip was incredible. He not only got to see a part of the continent he had never seen before, but he also developed a keen playing style. "On that trip, my entire game suddenly developed," wrote Russell in

Go Up for Glory. "Perhaps it was the security of knowing I was going to college."

Whatever the case, he was finally on his way to becoming a champion. The USF scholarship was the break of a lifetime for Russell. Everything was included: room, board, tuition, and even books. The only thing he wouldn't get was spending money, which he could earn himself by working odd jobs such as waiting tables and washing dishes. Despite the fact that he had no idea where USF was, and, in fact, had no idea that the school even existed before DeJulio told him about it, Russell was about to gain the opportunity that changed his life.

Growing up black in a world where blacks were often treated poorly, Russell had his share of difficult times—moments of confusion about who he was, where he was going, and what it meant to be African American. At sixteen years of age, however, everything seemed to come into focus. One evening he went to bed as William Felton Russell the boy, and the next day everything had changed. In *Go Up for Glory,* Russell wrote, "I woke up the next morning proud—so very proud—to be a Negro. The pride has ever since been with me. I could not put my finger on what triggered this emotion. But it was there . . . Perhaps, in turn, it gave me the impetus to fight the power structure and go forward."

The Dons and Beyond

Russell began college in the fall of 1952. At that time, USF was a small school and it wasn't very well known in the San Francisco area, let alone in the United States. As far as basketball went, it was truly anonymous. The school had won the 1949 National Invitational Tournament (NIT), for decent teams that fail to make it to the National Collegiate Athletic Association's (NCAA) Tournament, but since then had been on a slide and hadn't had a winning season since 1950. The campus didn't even have its own gym.

A Black and White Decision

In the 1950s, when Russell played college ball, black players were few and far between. It wasn't because blacks didn't play ball as well as whites, however. It was because of racism. Schools and professional teams thought that they'd be ridiculed if they had more than one or two "token" black players on their teams. They were afraid fans would stop coming to games if blacks played. In some cases, they even believed in racial stereotypes and doubted that blacks could play as well as whites could.

The University of San Francisco was not like most schools, and in 1955 the Dons were one of just a few teams to include three black players in their starting lineup. The team stuck to its belief that all players were equal, and even had to stand behind those beliefs at times. In one well-known instance of harassment, the Dons traveled to Oklahoma City for a tournament. When they arrived at their hotel they were told that only whites could stay in the rooms and that blacks would have to stay elsewhere. Rather than give in to this racist segregation, the entire team left the hotel and roomed together in a nearby college dormitory.

Bill Russell during his days with the University of San Francisco Dons

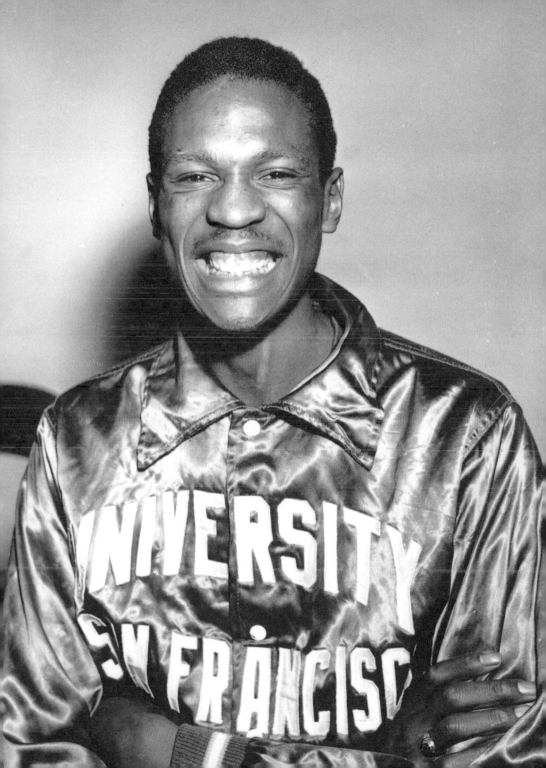

In the end, this attitude proved to be crucial to the Dons' success. They were a true team, one that refused to be split up by anything, including racial intolerance.

Russell was excited to get started. The USF scholarship was the one and only chance he was offered, and he was determined to excel. Hot off his all-star basketball tour through the Pacific Northwest, Russell had a new outlook on basketball. He had finally figured out how the game was played and had blossomed as a player. And, most important, he had discovered his main strength: defense.

As a freshman, Russell was six feet nine inches tall and 190 pounds. He was certainly big, but he had much to learn and, along with the other players his age, he started out with the freshman team.

The job of the freshmen coach, Ross Giudice, was to teach his players what it took to play at the collegiate level. Giudice worked specifically with Russell, as it was obvious how much raw talent the player had. They frequently played one-on-one ball together and Russell learned to employ the hook shot, in which he used one long arm to arc the ball high over his head before flicking it into the basket. He also learned to play the pivot, an offensive maneuver in which he would stand with his back to the basket, receive a high pass from a teammate, and then immediately send it to another player who would shoot it. He turned the act of dunking the ball into a deadly weapon, and made shot blocking his specialty. Thanks to Giudice and his own hard work, Russell improved rapidly. He quickly became a top prospect for USF's varsity team.

Meanwhile, off the court, Russell shared a dorm room with another basketball player, K. C. Jones, a sophomore player, a year ahead of Russell. The two had a rough start—neither boy was very talkative and it took awhile for them to get to know each other. Eventually, however, they became good friends, and Jones, who received $30 per month on top of his scholarship, began taking Russell out on the town, buying him small gifts, and bringing him

Stretching to his full length, Bill Russell goes for a field goal during a tournament game in Corvallis, Oregon, in March 1956, where he would score 21 points.

along everywhere he went. Neither player knew it then, but they would eventually become world-famous teammates on the Boston Celtics.

Varsity Star

Russell moved into his varsity position at the start of his sophomore year. He had grown about an inch as a freshman, and was now at his full height of six feet ten inches tall. Back in the 1950s, basketball players of this size were very rare. Most players were much shorter, and the ability to move quickly was valued far more than height. Russell, however, defied the stereotype of a "big" man. He was unusually fast and agile, and could jump so high that he could touch a point four feet above the rim. He was like a giant spring. When the ball went up, you could bet your last dollar that Russell would bring it down.

The USF varsity coach was Phil Woolpert. Woolpert, a future Hall of Famer himself, had been skeptical about Russell's talents when they first met. He wasn't so sure Hal DeJulio had been right when he'd said Russell was exactly what the team needed in the center position. With this in mind, it wasn't surprising that Russell and Woolpert had trouble clicking when Russell joined the varsity team in 1953. Woolpert had an entirely different outlook on the game than did Russell. Woolpert thought the budding talent should work on his offensive skills, especially his shooting technique. On one hand, he didn't think Russell's defensive abilities alone would win games for the San Francisco Dons. Russell, on the other hand, had been content with becoming the best defensive player ever. He thought that as long as he could bring down the ball and get it to his teammates, the Dons would win. As it turned out, a combination of both defense and offense was what the team really needed, and that's what Russell finally delivered.

The Dons entered the 1953–1954 season unranked in the National Collegiate Athletic Association. Preseason rankings are standard in college basketball and give opposing teams an idea about how basketball experts feel they stand up to the competition.

The USF Dons hoist Bill Russell
up on their shoulders in
celebration of their winning the
NCAA Tournament in 1956.

Run for the Title

Because the Dons were unranked, most people doubted they would do very well. Other teams were far too skilled for the Dons to compete with, they said. Besides, it was highly unlikely that the situation could be turned around in only one season. Still, several close observers noted that with K. C. Jones and Russell, the Dons could surprise everyone and could make a run for the title.

In the first game of the season, USF faced the University of California Bears. The Bears, unlike the Dons, were well respected. They were ranked tenth in the country, with just nine teams across the nation performing better than they did. They had a six-foot seven-inch, all-American center named Bob McKeen, and four excellent ball players to back him up. The outlook was grim: Such a tough contest this early in the season could easily prove disastrous for the Dons.

But USF would have none of the hype. From the moment the ball went up to signal the start of play, they dominated the game. Russell bounced all over the court and crushed McKeen. In the end, the Dons won the game 51–33. Would 1953 be USF's year?

The answer, unfortunately, came just before the very next game. Lining up to play Fresno State, USF was set on winning. The Dons were still full of adrenaline coming off their upset victory over California. They were totally hyped.

Then, disaster struck. For no apparent reason, as he prepared for the game in the locker room, K. C. Jones's appendix burst. You can't play basketball with a ruptured appendix—in fact, you really can't do anything. Jones, one of the team's top scorers, was out for that game and for the season. Suddenly the tables had been turned. The Dons went from complete elation at beating one of the country's best teams, to instant depression at losing one of their best players. Jones's illness crushed their hopes for a national championship.

Despite the circumstances, USF won the game against Fresno State, but the team just wasn't the same without Jones. They went on to

USF's other star player, K.C. Jones, shoots a basket during a semifinal game in March 1955, in which the Dons eventually beat Colorado, 62–50.

win twelve more games in the following months, and finished the season with fourteen wins and seven losses—a remarkable record considering what the team had been through. It was USF's first winning season in years, and, largely because of Russell, the Dons became the country's top defensive team. Thanks to Russell's superb shot blocking, the Dons allowed opponents an average of just 55 points per game. In basketball, where 100-plus points per game is not uncommon, that's quite a feat. Meanwhile, perhaps so as not to let his coach down, Russell managed to score a few points himself along the way. He even had one three-game swing in which he scored 25, 32, and 31 points. Russell was improving and so was the team, but K. C. Jones, still recovering, was its missing link.

With the start of the 1954–1955 season, Jones was back. Russell, now a junior, was also in the lineup, and the team—which included stars like Jerry Mullen, Stan Buchanan, and Hal

Perry—was on a mission. It was time to show the world just how talented they really were.

As expected, the season started with a bang: USF thrashed California State University 84–55. Unexpectedly, Russell displayed a new edge to his game, scoring 39 points—a new school record. The team was hot, and Russell was on fire.

The second game proved to be more of the same. In a nine-point victory over Loyola University, the Dons looked every bit the championship team they thought they were. Russell continued to drop the ball through the net and blocked anything that came near the basket. To put it mildly, it didn't look good for the opposition.

The following week, however, the Dons crashed. When they looked at their schedule and saw they were scheduled to face the University of California at Los Angeles (UCLA), they knew they were in for a tough game.

UCLA was well known in basketball circles. There was no doubt that the school had a great team. Their main point scorer, Willie Naulls, was destined for an all-star season.

Unfortunately for Russell and the Dons, their worst nightmare came true. Naulls had a fantastic game. He had no trouble taking the ball to the hoop over Russell. He scored almost at will. In the end, UCLA won the match 47–40, and the blame fell on Russell, who earlier had felt as if he was on top of the world. "I blew it all by myself," Russell wrote in *Go Up for Glory*.

The regret was short-lived. The following week the Dons faced UCLA again, and this time they refused to lie down and die. Russell and his teammates won by 12 points. A reporter for a local newspaper, the *San Francisco Chronicle*, wrote, "It might easily have been a rout . . . Don center Bill Russell [who scored 28 points] and his four mates completely dominated play." UCLA had been ranked number six in the country. The Dons were back on top, and, as it turned out, this time there was no going back.

By the end of the season, the Dons had won twenty-six straight games, never losing a contest

> **Tournament Stats**
>
> **B**ill Russell dominated play throughout the 1955 NCAA Tournament, and by the time USF defeated Philadelphia's LaSalle College 77–63 in the Finals, he had solidified his place as a force to be reckoned with. Bill, who had blocked countless shots and scored a record 118 points in five postseason games, was named Most Valuable Player of the tournament. He was also named an all-American— an honor given to a select few of the country's top basketball players.

that season after their second bout with UCLA. They crushed other college teams and, fittingly, they also won the 1955 NCAA Championship. The team had broken new ground for basketball by being the first championship team in NCAA history to start three black players in the final game. They were, without a doubt, one of the best teams in college basketball.

Russell so overpowered his teammates during his junior year that officials decided

A backboard eye view of Bill Russell
showing how he scores baskets, taken in
February 1956

something had to be done. As a defensive player, he was able to block shots like no one else had before him. When he played offense, he was dunking almost at will, and was such a good jumper that he would often catch his teammates' shots in midair and redirect them to the hoop to score. His teammates had to move the ball only toward the basket and leave the rest up to Russell.

NCAA officials were so worried that big men like Russell would change the game forever that they decided to alter the rules following the Dons' first victorious season. One new rule made it illegal for a player to touch the ball as it traveled toward the basket following a teammate's shot. This action became known as offensive goaltending. Teams who were caught doing this would be forced to give the ball to the opposition and any points scored from the illegal play would be disallowed.

A second new rule, known as the Bill Russell Rule, widened the free-throw lane from six feet to twelve feet. Because offensive players are permitted to stand in the free-throw lane for just three seconds at a time before they must step out, with the smaller lane, big players tended to stand just outside the paint and wait for the ball. Then, when they got it, they would be right near the basket and scoring would be a cinch. With the rule change, such players—including Russell—were forced to stand farther away from the basket.

Because he was such a good jumper, the Bill Russell Rule did absolutely nothing to stop Russell. As soon as the 1955–1956 season began, it was obvious that the Dons would continue their winning streak. And despite the fact that they still didn't have their own home court, they won again and again, ultimately finishing the year undefeated with a record of twenty-nine wins and no losses, including an 83–71 pummeling of Iowa State for the 1956 NCAA Championship. All told, since that first loss to UCLA in 1954, USF had won fifty-five straight games. Russell, named to the all-American team for the second year in a row,

In Print

The final game of the 1955 NCAA Tournament saw two great players lead two great teams. LaSalle College was directed by four-time all-American senior Tom Gola. It was commonly believed that Gola was the best basketball athlete ever to grace a court. USF had Bill Russell, the country's top defensive player, as well as a lethal point scorer. When the two met in the championship match, it was anybody's guess what would happen.

What did happen, of course, went down in history as Bill Russell's first major championship

victory. And for the record, a reporter for the *San Francisco Examiner*, in his write-up after the game, noted the following: ". . . if Gola is the 'greatest player of all time,' then 'Bill Russell the remarkable' is greater than the greatest."

had finished his collegiate career, but now it was time to move on. Not only had he established himself as the NCAA's most outstanding player, but he was also named Player of the Year in 1956, and averaged more than 20 points per game—a total of 1,636 points during his college career.

Extracurricular Activities

Russell kept very busy over the summer following the 1954–1955 season. He brought his leaping skills to USF's varsity track and field team. He said he joined the squad for fun, claiming he wanted the letter jacket that came with being a member of the team. High jumping, not surprisingly, became his specialty, and he soon found himself competing against some of the world's best jumpers, and still doing quite well.

Also that summer, Russell journeyed to Washington, D.C., to meet President Dwight Eisenhower. He had been invited to the White House to represent collegiate basketball at a conference on physical fitness. Russell, his

61

father, his stepmother (Charles Russell remarried after Katie's death), and Russell's girlfriend, Rose, piled into a car and drove across the country for the event.

Afterward, on the return trip to San Francisco, Russell and his crew dropped in to to see family in Louisiana. He hadn't driven through the Deep South in years, and had forgotten just how different a world it was from California. Suddenly, out of the spotlight of basketball fame, away from Washington, D.C., and thousands of miles from USF, Russell realized that he was just another black-skinned youth in potentially dangerous territory. He and his family had no rights. Whites treated them like they were animals. The experience would stay with Russell forever. "It made an impression," wrote Russell in *Go Up for Glory*. "A deep one. It made one that may have affected the rest of my days."

The NBA Draft

After winning his second NCAA Championship as one of the Dons, the unthinkable was

Celtics co-owners Walter A. Brown and Lou Pieri look on as Bill Russell signs on to play with their team, making him the highest paid rookie to date.

actually happening to Russell. Here he was, a one-time klutz who could barely catch a basketball let alone block one or put one through the hoop, and now he was the center of attention in the 1956 NBA draft. Scouts for various professional teams had watched Russell play over the past two years and they wanted him to play on their teams.

One such team, the Boston Celtics, was particularly interested. Russell had developed a reputation as the game's best collegiate center, so Red Auerbach, the Celtics' coach, sent a scout to observe his skills. The scout's opinion was mixed. Russell, he said, was way too skinny. There was no doubt he would be hammered and pushed around by tougher NBA players. He couldn't shoot to save his life. But, he added, there was one more thing: Russell was the best darn basketball player he had ever seen play the game.

Auerbach was convinced. He decided to sign Russell to his team. When the draft rolled around in May 1956, he went to work. Teams took turns picking players, and six other teams would be picking ahead of Boston. There was no chance that Russell would still be available when the Celtics had their turn, so Auerbach had to get crafty.

He approached the manager of the St. Louis Hawks, who would be picking second, and offered him a deal. If St. Louis would pick

64   Bill Russell gets a rebound during the gold medal game against the USSR during the 1956 Olympic Games in Melbourne, Australia.

Russell then trade him to the Celtics, he said, then Boston would give them two of their best players: Ed Macauley and Cliff Hagan. St. Louis agreed, and the deal was set.

The Olympics

Before he went to the pros, however, Russell excelled as an Olympiad. He had been invited to the 1956 Summer Olympic Games in Melbourne, Australia, as a member of the U.S. Olympic basketball team.

In order for the eleven Olympic players to adjust to being on the same court together as a team, they needed to practice. To accomplish this, they lined up a number of exhibition games in the United States before leaving for Australia—contests that didn't count, but that served as great practice.

At one of these exhibition games, a competition against an all-star team in College Park, Maryland, Russell finally got to meet Red Auerbach, his future coach. He hadn't negotiated the contract with the Celtics yet, and this was his chance. Their first meeting would take place after the game. Now, Russell had to play ball. And Auerbach, for the very first time, would be watching.

As he later recalled in a 1968 interview with *Sports Illustrated*, Russell's performance wasn't exactly stellar. "He was horrible," said Auerbach. "He was awful. I thought, God, I've traded Ed Macauley and Cliff Hagan for this guy! I sat there with my head in my hands. He came over to see me after the game. He said he wanted to apologize—he'd never played like that. I looked at him and said I hoped he was right because if his play that night was any indication of his ability, then I was a dead pigeon."

Nevertheless, as the two ate a postgame dinner together, they made an informal agreement. Russell would receive $22,500 for his rookie year, minus a small percentage because he would miss the first two months of the Celtics' season while he played for the U.S. Olympic team. (At the time the figure represented the highest salary ever paid to an

Bill Russell, with his then wife Rose, speaks with Celtics coach Red Auerbach during a Celtics game on the eve of Russell's signing with the NBA team from Boston.

NBA player.) He would return from Melbourne, plan his wedding to Rose, get married, and then sign the official contract with the Celtics to start his professional career.

The Olympics went just as everyone had expected. The U.S. team, which had won top honors in every basketball tournament since the game was first introduced as an Olympic sport in 1936, took home the gold. Along the way they beat teams from the Philippines, Japan, Uruguay, and Thailand. In the final game against the Soviet Union, Russell outplayed a seven-foot-tall Russian center as he led his team to an 89–55 victory and the gold medal. The Olympics, said Russell, were "one of the biggest thrills of my life."

Later, back in Oakland, on December 9, 1956, Russell and Rose were married. Nearly 300 people squeezed into the church for the ceremony. Just a week after their honeymoon, the couple flew to Boston. It was time to sign the contract that would make Bill Russell a Celtic.

The Boston Celtics

Before Russell joined the team, the Boston Celtics had never won an NBA championship. They took second place three times between 1952 and 1956—the years Russell played for USF—but in each instance couldn't finish first.

They did have many excellent players. One playmaker in particular, Bob Cousy, a six-foot one-inch guard, was the best dribbler in the league. He could go behind the back in the blink of an eye and was famous for his laser-accurate, no-look passes. It was Cousy and Auerbach, the team's energetic coach, who had led the team, but now it was up to Russell to take them to the next level.

Coach Red Auerbach congratulates star player Bill Russell on his 10,000th point during a game against the Baltimore Bullets on December 12, 1964.

When Russell finally arrived in Boston after his honeymoon and suited up, the Celtics were already two months into their season. They were doing quite well, too. In fact, they were on top of the standings, leading the league. For Russell, it was an awkward situation. He wasn't certain he was really needed. How could he help this team if they were already doing so well?

On top of that, he was the only black man on the team. He knew that many fans would judge him only by his skin color. No matter how well he did on the court, he would be African American to them, and therefore would be considered inferior by some.

He had to prove himself. Many writers, coaches, players, and other critics felt that he didn't have the offensive skills to make it in the NBA. They knew that he could hold his own defensively, but they highly doubted that he could score points when they were needed most. His strategy was the same as it had always been: Russell wanted to play the game he loved for himself alone.

"I knew what I was doing. I was going to go out and play my guts out and prove a point—to me, just to me. In all my life, I've never done anything I didn't do flat out—right or wrong—and I don't know any other way to do it," Russell wrote in *Go Up for Glory.*

Russell was not about to listen to his critics. He decided that he would do what he did best—play the center position. He also decided that he would do what Auerbach had asked him to do when he'd signed—rebound or block the ball and get it to the team's shooters.

And with a controlled effort, that's exactly what he did. In his relatively short rookie season, Russell quickly became the best defensive center ever to play the game. He would go up for countless rebounds, and come down with the ball nearly every time. He would then whip it to a teammate as he broke for the opponent's basket, and the Celtics would score. With Russell's efforts, the team was a finely tuned scoring machine.

Wilt Chamberlain said in *Sporting News*, "The best rebounder I've ever seen is Bill Russell. There's no doubt about it. When they needed a rebound, Bill Russell went and got it for them. He made all the difference in the world."

Despite the fact that he was not a major scoring threat that first year, he was the key to almost every point they made. After all, the Celtics had to get the ball in order to have a

Bob Cousy of the Celtics goes
for a layup against the
Syracuse Nationals during the
Eastern Division playoffs at
Boston Garden in March 1957.

chance to score, and getting the ball was Russell's specialty. (Although Russell will be remembered for his incredible defensive skills, he was no slacker on offense, either: He scored a total of 14,522 points during his NBA career.)

As the Celtics sailed toward their first NBA Championship with Russell at the helm, word got around that he might be named the league's Rookie of the Year. After all, he was so overpowering on defense that he was changing the way the game was played. By turning shot blocking into a precise art— timing his leaps perfectly and not only stopping shots but redirecting them to teammates in the same motion—he was single-handedly ruining other teams' offenses. Players who had before never hesitated to take the ball and loft it up toward the basket, were intimidated by Russell and afraid to shoot. And even when they did shoot, they were often so worried Russell would swat it away, that they missed the basket anyway.

By making defense his strongest asset, Russell forced other teams to emphasize defense as well. Otherwise, when they played the Celtics, they were bound only for defeat.

When the playoffs finally began in March 1957, the Celtics were practically unstoppable. The team stormed through the Eastern Division Championships by beating Syracuse, then, in the Finals, faced off against the St. Louis Hawks, the same team that had traded Russell in the draft. Here was Russell's chance to show the Celtics just how great a deal they got when they swapped Hagan and Macauley for him.

The championship game was a best-of-seven series, so the first team to win four games would win the title. After six games, the two teams were tied with three wins each, so it all came down to one final battle on April 13, 1957.

For dichard Celtics fans, that day will never be forgotten. Russell and his teammates fought to the very end. By regulation, the game was tied. After the first overtime, the score remained equal. Then, finally, as the last seconds ticked off the clock during overtime, the Celtics held a two-point lead. They won the game, 125–123. For the first time ever, the Celtics were the champions of the world!

A Rookie, but Not Rookie of the Year

By all accounts, Russell's first season in the NBA was spectacular. On defense, he served as the Celtics' personal wall, swatting away shots as though they were flies. He also snagged 943 rebounds. As an offensive player, despite all the criticism that he wasn't up to NBA standards, he sunk 43 percent of his shots. He had 706 points, for an average of 14.7 points per game, in a season that was shortened by two months. He was, without a doubt, the key to the Celtics' championship.

Yet despite his success on the court, and the resulting success of his team, Russell did not win the NBA's Rookie of the Year award. That honor went to his offense-minded teammate, Tommy Heinsohn, a six-foot seven-inch forward from Holy Cross College. Heinsohn was the Celtics' go-to man on offense, and he did a lot for the team. But many felt that Russell should have won the award instead. There are a number of theories about why he didn't, but many felt it was because he only played for part of the year. Other people thought racism was to blame. Others thought there was nothing suspicious about the decision at all.

In the 1950s, when Russell began his NBA career, racism was rampant throughout the United States. Many blacks and whites did not get along, and in many places blacks were not allowed the same rights as whites. Segregation—official and unofficial—was common. But as a member of the Celtics, said Russell, skin color did not matter. All Celtics players were equal, and every player treated every other player in the same manner. They were athletes and would judge each other based on their athletic performance, not on the color of their skin. They were teammates, and would stick together no matter what, all the way to the world championships.

Throughout his career in the NBA, Bill Russell displayed an artful touch around the basket whether he was scoring, rebounding, or blocking shots.

Whatever the case, if not receiving the award bothered Russell he didn't show it at the time. For him, basketball was all about the team, not about individual honors. He had one concern only, and that was helping the Celtics win championships.

The Finals

In his second season—and his first full year as a Celtic—Russell had similar good fortune. Until, the Finals, that is.

As they did in 1957, the Celtics romped through the regular season as though they owned the court. They won the Eastern Division title for the second year in a row, waltzed through the playoffs, then met the St. Louis Hawks for a repeat of the previous year's Finals series.

Then, in Game 3, with the series tied, Russell jumped for a rebound and came down hard. His ankle had given out. He thought it was merely sprained and tried to continue playing, but the pain was too great. Later, doctors' tests showed that it was broken, and

Russell was officially out for the series and for the season.

It was exactly the "break" that St. Louis needed. Although Boston put up a great fight in the next several games, they couldn't pull off the championship. St. Louis won in Game 6, and the Celtics' hopes of winning back-to-back championships were dashed. Russell, despite having been named the NBA's Most Valuable Player for the season, and despite his pride in his team's valiant effort, was dejected. He had won championships in each of the previous three years—two in college and one in the pros—as well as a gold medal with the Olympic team. Losing was not a part of his vocabulary, nor would it be for the next eight years.

The Streak

Following the 1958 championship loss, Russell's Celtics began what was then and what continues to be considered the greatest team sports accomplishment in history. To put it simply, they were unbeatable.

At the start of the 1958–1959 season, two key players joined the team: future Hall of Famer Sam Jones and K. C. Jones, Russell's old roommate and teammate from USF. The combination proved lethal. With Russell anchoring the Celtics machine beneath the basket, the team regrouped and won their second world championship in three years.

The next year they did it again, defeating St. Louis in the Finals. In 1960–1961 they made it three in a row, and in 1961–1962 they won number four.

It would be easy to go through all the games and list all the statistics for every player who stepped on the court, but that would just take away from the true significance of what the Celtics did in the late 1950s and throughout the 1960s. Let's just say that, for all intents and purposes, the team was absolutely unstoppable. There were other players on the Boston team in addition to Russell, and they also made it happen: Cousy, Sam Jones and K. C. Jones, Heinsohn, and an incredibly hardworking

During his thirteen years with the Boston Celtics, Russell scored many second-chance points—baskets made after grabbing rebounds.

85

In Between Seasons

After the 1959 season, Russell began an annual tradition that for him proved to be one of the most rewarding aspects of his career. He traveled to cities in western and southern Africa, including Liberia. He considered Africa his homeland and wanted to see where he and his family originated. He also went to spread friendship and goodwill, and spent most of his time traveling from village to village, meeting children and introducing them to the game of basketball. The youngsters loved him, even though the language barrier prevented any conversation between them. Instead, basketball became their common tongue.

Then, in July 1963, the summer after the Celtics won their fifth consecutive championship, Russell journeyed to Jackson, Mississippi—the heart of the Deep South—to teach a three-day basketball clinic to area schoolchildren. At that time, Jackson was not a

Starting in 1959, Bill Russell made annual goodwill trips to South Africa and visited villages like this one on a Bantu reservation in North Transvaal.

safe place to go if you were black, and the fact that Russell was famous made his trip that much more dangerous. Just before he left Boston, he received death threats from racists.

Russell refused to back down and went anyway. He knew how important it was for him to stand up to the bigotry and go forward with the clinic. Later, in *Go Up for Glory*, he remembered, "No one was going to drive me out . . . It was just something I *had* to do."

player named John Havlicek. Still each was at his best when working with the team, moving the ball down the court for a basket, or uniting to stop the opposition in its tracks on defense. Taken as a whole, the group was like no other team in the history of the game.

Throughout the Celtics' championship streak, which included eleven titles in thirteen seasons between 1957 and 1969, defense was the name of the game. With Russell at center, the Celtics evolved into the best defensive team the NBA had ever seen. They scored scads of points, especially with sharp shooters like Sam Jones leading the way, but every year it was their defensive playing style that won the games. Russell was known as the defense's most important component.

The Wilt Factor

Another common thread to the Celtics' streak was Wilt Chamberlain, the league's most dangerous offensive threat, and Russell's biggest challenge on defense. Chamberlain could score 50 points in

Philadelphia 76er (and fellow legend) Wilt Chamberlain gets one over Bill Russell during the Eastern Conference Championship in April 1967.

a game and hardly break a sweat. He was league MVP four times between 1958 and 1968. A tall, incredibly strong player, Chamberlain was gifted when it came to playing basketball. When Chamberlain and Russell met on the court—and they faced off in eight playoffs, not to mention countless regular-season games—it was like two thunderstorms colliding. The whole court shook when they battled beneath the hoop.

The first time the two superstars met was in the Boston Garden on November 7, 1959. Before the game, Chamberlain had been averaging 45 points per night. But as a sign of things to come for the next decade, Russell stood up to Chamberlain like no one else in the league could have. He scored 22 points and snatched 38 rebounds as Boston won the game, 115–106. Chamberlain, meanwhile, grabbed 35 rebounds and scored 30 points. These were big numbers by anyone's standards, but they were not great enough to get the job done. In the years to come, these point totals became normal. Chamberlain would almost always have a good game, but when it mattered, his efforts usually fell short to win. The Celtics won seven of their eight series games against Chamberlain and his teams, and Russell ultimately went home the champion. "Chamberlain was my greatest challenge," wrote Russell. "He won his awards. I won mine. To me, the great awards were the championships."

Ironically enough, Russell sometimes became sick to his stomach prior to an important game. John Havlicek, now a writer for *Sports Illustrated*, said in a 1968 article for the magazine, "[Russell] used to throw up all the time before a game, or at halftime—a tremendous sound, almost as loud as his laugh. He doesn't do it much now, except when it's an important game or an important challenge for him—someone like Chamberlain, or someone coming up that everyone's touting. It's a welcome sound, too, because it means he's keyed up for the game, and around the locker room we grin and say, 'Man, we're going to be alright tonight.'"

The rivalry between Bill Russell and Wilt Chamberlain sometimes found its way off the court, too. In one famous instance, before the start of the 1965–1966 season, Chamberlain signed a contract with San Francisco for $100,000. The Celtics, meanwhile, had offered Russell just $70,000 for the year. Russell, feeling he must be worth more than Chamberlain since he'd led his team to seven straight world championships, turned down the offer. His counter offer was $100,001. The Celtics agreed. For that year, anyway, Russell made one dollar more than Chamberlain did.

Player-Coach

When the 1965–1966 season rolled to a close and the Celtics had secured their eighth championship in a row, Auerbach decided that it was finally time to call it quits as the team's coach. He would move up to become its manager, and, if his star player would agree, Russell would step in as the first black man ever to coach an NBA team.

92

After a stellar career on the court, Bill Russell went on to coach the Sacramento Kings.

Russell, a natural leader, agreed, and beginning with the 1966–1967 season he served as both the Celtics' coach, and as one of their players. The team did well and looked strong as they approached the playoffs. Then, for the first time in nine years, they lost in the Eastern Division Finals to Chamberlain's 76ers. It was the first time since 1956 that the Celtics had not made it to the NBA Finals. Russell felt terrible. He hated losing. He had been contemplating retirement following that season, but now it was out of the question. He had to go out on top.

The Celtics stormed back the following year and, in the semifinals, dispatched Chamberlain and the 76ers. Russell played one of his best games, holding Chamberlain to just one shot in the second half of the game. Later in the Finals, the Celtics beat the Los Angeles Lakers for the championship.

The next year their good fortune continued. But, again, they had to get by Chamberlain, who was playing with the Los Angeles Lakers. In Game 7 of the Finals, with just a few seconds remaining, Chamberlain was out with an injury, and the Celtics were in the lead by two points. A Lakers player had the ball and took a shot from beneath the basket, but Russell blocked the ball and the Celtics won the game. For the second year in a row, the eleventh time in thirteen years, the Celtics were NBA champions. Russell decided to retire. He was ready to move on.

A True Champion

With his official retirement, Russell said good-bye to the game of basketball—at least as a player. He packed up his belongings and drove his speedy Lamborghini across the country to Los Angeles, where he settled in Hollywood. Shortly before he had also decided to separate from his wife Rose. Russell was now searching for a new life.

In Los Angeles, he took up other sports such as golf, did a little acting for small parts on television shows and advertisements, and relaxed. Eventually, though, he became tired of staying in one place all the time. Life on the road as a Celtic, while often frustrating and full of long, lonely nights alone in strange hotel

rooms, was electric by comparison, and he
required a more action-oriented lifestyle. He
decided to join the college lecture circuit, and
began traveling around the country to speak at
universities about subjects relevant to
students. He was a famous, well-respected
man, and people both young and old were
interested in what he had to say. They were
fascinated by how successful he had been
throughout his career.

Russell also began doing commentary for
several television networks. He worked at
televised basketball games and offered his take
on the players, the teams, and the contests
themselves. At one point, he even had his own
radio show. Russell was keeping very busy,
much the way he did as a player. It was just
what he needed.

Then, in 1973, the owner of the Seattle
Supersonics called him. He needed a new coach
and general manager to take hold of his struggling
team. Russell, at first reluctant to reenter the
game, eventually agreed to take the position. He

Bill Russell answers reporters' questions at a press conference after having been named head coach of the Sacramento Kings.

moved to Seattle and stayed with the Sonics for four years, building the team into a top contender for the NBA championship. Although he didn't win any titles with the Supersonics, he did leave his mark: Just two years after he left, they won it all. Russell returned to coaching once again in 1987 to lead the Sacramento Kings, but remained there for only one year.

Life Off the Court

Between coaching stints, Russell has lived a fairly private life. He usually refuses to give interviews to the press, and he prefers to hunker down at home in Seattle and go golfing with friends. He's been remarried twice since his 1973 divorce from Rose. His children are grown and have careers of their own.

The Boston Celtics decided to retire Russell's number in 1972. Russell, ever the team player, couldn't stand the idea of a public ceremony in Boston Garden honoring his individual contributions—he played for the Celtics, he said, not for the fans. On these grounds, he refused to attend. The ceremony was postponed, and eventually, after much prodding by Auerbach, Russell agreed to a private celebration with some of his teammates. His number was retired, and today it hangs in the rafters at Celtics home games.

In another controversial ceremony, Russell was enshrined in the NBA Hall of Fame

on April 28, 1975. He was the first black player to be inducted, but he didn't want any part of it. He felt the Hall of Fame, as an institution, was racist, run by white people for white people. He also didn't understand the point. In the same way he felt as though autographs were silly (he refused to give autographs throughout his career, preferring instead to shake hands or talk with fans), he believed that being inducted into the Hall of Fame was all a show. Although it went on without him, he refused to participate in the ceremony.

Russell was never one to follow. On the court or off, he always led the way—for his team, for athletes, even for his race. By standing up for the things in which he believed, and by persevering in spite of obstacles in his path when it appeared he had nowhere else to go, he set a positive example for people everywhere. In the same way he changed basketball, making defense an important part of the game, Russell confronted racism and bigotry in his own unique way. He would deal

Over the course of his incredible career, Bill Russell played and coached his way into the ranks of the greatest basketball legends of all time.

with it and then turn away. He refused to be pushed around by anyone, and would sooner walk out of a segregated business, or ignore the courtside jeering and concentrate on winning, than confront an issue that he felt was unnecessary. Although it may have occasionally seemed like a contradiction, what Russell did was choose his battles carefully. He would never want to allow a situation, such as fans jeering during a game, to have more power than it deserved. Looking back at one of the greatest winners ever, it's obvious that he always knew what he was doing.

glossary

assist   A pass from one player to another that leads directly to a basket.

autobiography   The story of a person's life as written or told by that person.

bigotry   Intolerance of other people's opinions or beliefs.

center   Usually the tallest member on a team's starting unit; the player most responsible for plays closest to the basket, including rebounding, scoring, and shot blocking.

collegiate   Having to do with college.

contract   An official, legal agreement between a player and a team.

discrimination   Treating a person or people differently for reasons other than merit, such as skin color, sex, or age.

draft   The action of choosing new players from college to play on professional NBA teams.

forward   One of two players flanking the center, usually on offense. Forwards play close to the basket, and must be good shooters and rebounders. They are usually taller than guards, but shorter than centers.

free throw   An uncontested shot, worth one point, taken by a player who has been fouled. The number of shots depend on the situation of the foul.

fundamentals   Of, or relating to, essential structure, function, or facts; basic rules.

offensive   Of, or relating to, a team in possession of the ball.

overtime   An extra period played when a game ends in a tie.

pick-up game   Unofficial basketball game organized for anyone who wants to play.

preseason   Games that take place before the regular season begins.

racism   The belief that one race is superior to another.

104

rebound   To retrieve the ball as it comes from the rim or backboard, taking possession of it for either team.

rookie   Player in his or her first professional season.

varsity   Team of the best players in a school.

for more information

ESPN
506 Second Avenue
Suite 2100
Seattle, WA 98104
Web site: http://www.espn.com

Naismith Memorial Basketball Hall of Fame
1150 West Columbus Avenue
Springfield, MA 01105
(413) 781-6500
(877) 4-HOOPLA (446-6752)
Web sites: http://www.basketballhalloffame.com
          http://www.hoophall.com

Sports Illustrated
P.O. Box 60001
Tampa, FL 33660-0001
(800) 528-5000
Web site: http://www.sportsillustrated.com

Web Sites

Bill Russell—NBA.com
http://www.nba.com/history/russell_bio.html

The Naismith Memorial Basketball Hall of Fame
http://www.hoophall.com

NBA.com
http://www.nba.com

The Official Web Site of the Boston Celtics.
http://www.celtics.com

for further reading

Bjarkman, Peter C. *The Boston Celtics Encyclopedia*. Champaign, IL: Sports Publishing, Inc. 1999.

Nichols, John. *The History of the Boston Celtics*. Mankato, MN: Creative Education, 2001.

Russell, Bill, and William McSweeny. *Go Up For Glory*. New York: Coward-McCann, 1966.

Russell, Bill, and David Falkner. *Russell Rules: Eleven Lessons on Leadership from the Twentieth Century's Greatest Winner*. New York: Dutton, 2001.

Shaughnessy, Dan. *Ever Green: The Boston Celtics: A History in the Words of Their*

Players, Coaches, Fans and Foes, from 1946 to the Present. New York: St. Martin's Press, 1990.

Smith, Ron. *The Ultimate Encyclopedia of Basketball.* New York: Carlton Books, 1996.

index

About the Author

Chris Hayhurst is a writer living in northern Colorado.

Photo Credits

Cover, p. 17 © Dick Raphael; p. 4 © Herb Scharfman/TimePix; p. 10 © John G. Zimmerman/ TimePix; p. 13 © Hank Walker/TimePix; pp. 30–31, 39, 42–43, 56–57, 71, 89, 98 © AP Wide World Photos; p. 46–47 © Sam Goldstein/Corbis; pp. 50–51, 65, 68, 74–75 © Bettmann/Corbis; pp. 60, 93 © Basketball Hall of Fame; pp. 63, 87 © Hulton Archive; pp. 80–81, 84 © Larry C. Morris/ New York Times Co./Archive Photos; p. 100 © John Sotomayor/New York Times Co./Archive Photos.

Series Design and Layout

Geri Giordano